Master Handbook of Sound Healing

Copyright © 2019 Thomas Orr Anderson
All rights reserved.

No part of this book may be reproduced or distributed in any manner whatsoever without explicit written permission from the author except in the case of brief quotations embodied in articles or reviews.

Cover design and illustrations by
Thomas Orr Anderson

Books in the Sound Therapy Foundations Series:

0. Master Handbook of Sound Healing
1. Physics of Sound & Vibration
2. Dimensions, Spaces, & Symbiotic Fields

Published by SwallowsItself Media

ThomasOrrAnderson.com

ISBN: 9781797471860

The
Master
asked...

What do you hear?

The
Student
answered...

Chapters

-1. Preface
0. Zero
1. One 2. Two 3. Three
4. Four 5. Phive 6. Six
7. Seven 8. Eight 9. Nine
10. Pendulum 11. Resonance
12. Time 13. Space 14. Dimensions
15. Attention 16. Qi 17. Obstruction
18. Environmental Space 19. Body Space
20. Emotional Space 21. Mind Space
22. Models & Maps
23. Circle... Cycle 24. Helix 25. Frequency
26. Breath
27. Mind... mind 28. Possibility
29. In Voluntary 30. Heart 31. Entrainment
32. Reflection 33. Boundary Conditions
34. Interference 35. Interference Patterns
36. Standing Waves
38. Quantization 39. Modes 40. Harmonics
41. Sound
42. Hearing 43. Body Hearing 44. Ear Hearing
45. Octave
46. Tones & Notes 47. Flavors of Tonal Spectrum
48. Divisions of Octave
49. Relativity of Frequency 50. Intervals
51. Whole Octave 52. Chord & Scale Geometry
53. Harmony 54. Life
55. Stickiness
56. Health
57. Drone 58. Groove
59. Meditation 60. Awakening 61. Treatment
62. Language 63. In Formation 64. In Coding
65. Self 66. Is 67. No Thing
68. Truth 69. Honesty 70. Ethics
71. Community 72. Waterfall Mountain
73. ? ? ? 74. Completeness
75. Practice 76. Student 77. Master
φ. Cues & Keys
π. Afterword
ω. About the Author

.

dedicated

to

Dr. Cayenne

- Leslie Alaxander Lacy -

whose

Generous Lessons

continue to

Teach

me

about

Nothing

.

Author's Preface

.
..
...
This

Book

is to a

Sound Practice

as a

Meditation Manual

is to a

Martial Art

.....
...
..
.

Sound Itself

Reveals

What

Is

only

Hinted

Herein

.

but...

in

Sound Itself,

It

Resounds...

That

Silent Center...

for

All

to

Hear

who

Listen

.

.
..
...
That
Which
Is

left out of this

Text

is

Widely available...

the

Science,

Techniques,

Art Forms,

Traditions
...
..
.

the
Vast array

of

Sound Knowledge
is
Woven around us

in
Webs

for
Each Student

to
Find...

Ever more clearly...

That One
Student's Path...

Tracing

Limited projections

of

Infinite Dimensional Form.

Included herein

is a

Circle,

the
Opposite sides

of

Which

Absorb
One
another,

Leaving only That

Silent Center,

Ever

Unwrit

.

Ode

from

Student
to
Master...

Only the Master can Read

What is meant to be said,

Yet is Not.

Student to Master...

Here are Notes

of

the
Journey...

the
Practice,

the
Work

.

.
..
...
From

Forms

to their

Center...

That Single Jump

NOW

is

Beginning to Listen
....
.....
...
..
.
.

The Student remembered...

What could be

more

Comical

than to

Entitle a book

such as

this...

for

the
Real

Master Handbook

is

Every Open Fist

.

I
Take full credit

for
Every stumble,
Mis-step and fumble,

but for
What's True Herein,

None can I take.

An
Honest Surfer

Takes None

for a
Wave,

as each
Surfer

is

A w a k e
.

- Thomas Orr Anderson
February 9, 2019
Sewanee, TN

0

Zero

Sound

is
Born

from
Silence.

To
Silence,

Sound returns.

Silence within Silence....

the

Center

of

Every Sound
.

Listen closely
to the
Myriad of sounds.

Arising
in
Awareness...

from
Whence

Do they come?

Fading

from
Awareness,

Where do they go?

Born from Silence,

Returning to Silence...

the
Eternal

Silent Center
.

.
..
...
Listen closely

to the

Myriad of sounds.

In their midst,

One Sound
is
Everywhere

Heard,

NOW and Always

...

Silent Center

in the

Midst of conditions.
...
..
.

One

Amidst

Silence,

a
Single pulse

Divides Time Now

as
Before and after.

Unexpected, is heard.

Remembered, survives only in reflection.

Leaving Now

Before arriving.

Two

Reflecting

in the
Mirror of Silence,

a
Second pulse is born.

Together as One,
the
Two make None.

Divided in Time,
the
Two are One.

One cycle...

Circle stretched in Time.

Three

One, two, three...

in
Three steps

Rhythm is born.

Did three come sooner or later

Than two came after One?

Two times to compare

Give birth to faster and slower.

Ratio is born...

The Essence of Earth and Heaven.

Four

Amidst
Four pulses,

Three intervals

are
Born...

the
Beginning of Harmony.

In
Space,

Three intervals

Give rise to Structure.

From
Three amidst four,

Myriad creations take Form.

5

Phive

From
Five is born

the
Golden Mean...
Essence of Synergy.

Woven as spirals

in
Forms of Life,

Self-creating,

Spiraling out

to
Infinity,

Spiraling in

to the
Silent Center

.

Two frequencies
United as One...

Make
a
Third...

as the
Difference

between the
Two.

If

Third is to second

as
Second to first...

the
Golden Spiral
does

by
Nature

Emerge
.

Six

The
Crystalline matrix
Born

of
Six arranged as One,

Yields

Structure
to
Grow and grow...

Stability

of
Infinite Form.

7

Seven

Six around One,

a
Perfect fit,

the
Seventh sits snug

in the
Middle...

Seed in a shell.

As if...

to
Represent the Unspeakable,

Seven equal divisions

Remain Unattainable

with the

Simple geometer's tools...

Straight lines and arcs....

Reminding us That...

in
Symbols,

a
Hint
is

All

We are Given.

Eight

Up, down...
Left, right...
Forward, back...

Space

in which

we
Move and measure

Here and there.

Three dimensions,
Six directions...

Enveloped as One

amidst

Eight corners.

Complete

Cycle

around a

Space...

Defines

a

Microcosm
.

2 x 2 x 2

Nine

Completing

an

Octave,

Return....

New

Beginning
.

Pendulum

A
Single push

Sets the Pendulum

to
Swinging.

If
Fast enough

Compared

to
Attention,

A single note is it singing.

The
Rate

of its
Pulse

Determined

by its
Length,

both
**Weak and strong
Pushes**

Set it
to
Dancing

in that
One natural rhythm.

Time is born.

We have our clock.

11

Resonance

Push

at the
Right time,

In sync

with its
Pulse,

So little work must you do

to
Awaken

its
One natural rhythm,

Effortlessly dancing

with
You
.

Push
Out of sync,

its
dancing

is
Rough

with
Wiggles, and jiggles, and junk.

Work as you may,
Push hard as you like...

Out of sync
Efforts

are

Sunk
.

Time

With
Memory and symbols,

Now

Able to count...

One, two, three, four,
and so on...

How many swings has the pendulum swung?

Thus...

Time is born.

Space

The
Pendulum
Swinging

To and fro

Gives birth

to

Here and there.

The
Harder we push,

the
Farther it goes.

Space

is the

Difference

.

Dimensions

Pointing to this,
Creating that...

Pointing up,
Creating down...

Thinking before,
Creating after...

Wanting more,
Creating less...

Believing in self,
Creating other...

Every
Conceivable change

Creates and defines
a
Dimension.

Time and Space...

Only a beginning lesson...

Teaching us clearly

that
there always are

Precisely as many dimensions

as
We conceive.

Attention

Stubbing a toe,

Attention does go...

Right to the spot

where it
Hurts.

A
Clap in the room
or
Snap of a twig...

Draws Attention

in

Space

.

.
A

Vibrating object

Touching your body...

Attention moves

to that
Place
.....
...
..
.

Attention

is the

I
That
I
Am,

Ever guided

by
That which draws It,

Traversing every dimension,

Silent,
Invisible,
Nowhere to be found...
yet
Always somewhere,

Its movements guided

by
Sound

.

Qi

Alive...

Sometimes ill,

Sometimes healthy.

Collaboration
of
Every process,

Team

Dancing in sync,

Cooperating...

Cooperation
.

Heart beating,

Lungs expanding... contracting,

Electrical pulses
in
Nervous channels,

Resonant waves
in the
Brain,

Blood and oxygen,

Nutrients and wastes...

Flowing

in

Harmonious cycles.

Amidst this
Beautiful Dance
of the
Many,

Attention
as
One,

Flows
Round and through and throughout.

Call It Qi if you like.

Where Attention goes...

Here
Do you find
It

.

17

Obstruction

Attention can go

from
Here to there,

yet sometimes

Not
in
Between.

This we call...

Obstruction
.

.
.
..
...
.....
....
Sound sneaks in,

Clears
the
Way.

Effortlessly

the
Path
is
Now
Open.

Wholeness restored...

the
Sum

of
Every path.

Environmental Space

The
Ancient Ones

had to
Listen

in
Every direction...

Just to survive.

The
common one

is
Boxed-in...

Attention bound

within
Rectangles...

Sleeping on rectangles,

Working and playing in rectangles,

Staring
into
One rectangle after another,

Day upon day.

Attention in Sound

Retains its flow...

Natural movements in arcs and spirals,

Fernlike,

Dancing

To and fro

in
Ever shifting currents.

Sound comes to save us...

Drawing Attention

in
Every direction,

Naturally flowing...

Every angle,
Every distance,
Every axis of twist...

Restoring

Full and Beautiful

Sense

of the
Dance

That
ever
Surrounds
.

Body Space

Right Now...

Where do you feel your body?

Your hands perhaps?

Or where you sit?

The knot in your back,
or
Pain in your shoulder?

Tickle of wind on your arm?

A second question,
Much harder to answer...

Where do you not feel your body?

The Student discovers...

These patterns so regular...

Carved in the map...

Trails of Attention in Body Space.

Yet
Sound comes to save us...

the
Simplest sound

Vibrating a blind spot,

Illuminates
Once hidden paths,

Despite having been ignored...

Concealed
in
Attention's shadow.

.
.
..
...
.....
....
Effortlessly,

Each path Lit

by the
Light of Sound...

Full Territory

Restored
....
.....
...
..
.
.

Emotional Space

Perhaps happy Now,
Sad in a moment...
Nostalgia, sorrow, or Joy,

a
Certain smell or taste,
or
Some feeling...

Remembering a favorite toy.

Just
as in the
Space of the room

or
that of our
Body within...

Attention traverses
Emotional Space

in
Cyclical paths without end.

Just
as in

each other
Space,

The common one is boxed-in...

in
Boxes of habit

Learned
from the others'

continually
Trying to win.

Hear One Sound

and
Feel this way,

Another and feel that...

Combinations
of
Tones and rhythms,

Harmonies, dynamics and timbre...

Evoking every emotion...

Illuminating

What was hid.

Pathways once obstructed...

Effortlessly

by
Sound...

Open

.

Mind Space

Thinking Now

of a
Ball, field, mouse, or a bat...

Idea
of
What to eat for dinner,

or the
Chair where Grandmother sat...

Attending

an
Object or thing,
Concept, phrase, or a book...

Ceaselessly passing
from
Point to point,

.

Tracing

Pathways,

Areas,

S p a c e s ,

Infinite

are

the

Realms

of

Mind

.

Yet...

Amidst the multitude,

There
is

a
Grand Pattern

of
Wholeness.

It cannot be captured

in
Any still frame,

for...

the
Whole

is

a
Dance...

is

Movement Itself.

That
Wholeness Illumined

in
Dancing Sound...

Such

is

the
Work.

The
Parts are many,

Whole is One.

Sing of It...

All who Listen

Return to the Center.

Such is the Work.

22
Models & Maps

The
Whole

cannot be

Pointed out,

Only the parts...

but

even at that,

Only

in

Models and maps.

The Student reminds us...

the
Map

is
Not

the
Territory.

We must be ever vigilant...

lest
We be fooled
into
Believing

that
Our pretty story

is the
Thing
.

The Student reminds us again...

The map is not the Territory.

Listen closely
and
Even closer...

the
Truth is Spoken
Now.

The
Song of the Ages
Every moment

is
Yours

to
Hear.

The Student reminds us...

Burn the map as you Arrive,

lest
another be
Fooled
by
Your pretty story.

Circle... Cycle

Relinquishing maps and models,

yet
One remains
Central
to
All Sound...

the Circle... the Cycle,

Essence of around.

Elemental repetition
Returning
to the
Start,

Defines

the
Silent Center
of the
Whole without a part.

24

Helix

The Cycle...

Repeated

Again and again,

Stretches

the
Circle
in
Time.

Helix is born...

as is the

Wave...

Helix shadow...

Projected Form.

Frequency

Counting each swing

of a
Pendulum Clock...

that
Count

we call
Time.

Comparing this count

to the
Number of cycles

in a
Cyclical system

and

Find

the
Ratio

of

System cycles
per
Unit Time.

The Student reminds us...

Frequency

is

How Frequently.

26

Breath

The
Central Cycle

of

Life

wherein

is
Found

the
Mystery of Will...

Attention elsewhere,

Breath goes on

Expanding, contracting
in
Rhythms...

Attention in Breath,

a
Force appears...

Pulls

the
Breath

toward that
Cycle Imagined...

as if
Imbued with Gravity,

the
Breath-That-Is

toward
That-Which-Is-Imagined.

Breathing fast,

One can Imagine

Soon
to
Breathe more slowly.

Breathing slowly,

can
Imagine

Arising rapid Breath.

A
Simple act of Attention

Draws
the
Breath cycle
of
Now

toward that
Breath Cycle Imagined.

That
Force,

Pulling
That-Which-Is

toward
a

Possibility

Held in Attention...

We call Will...

The Force

of

What-We-Are

.

Mind... mind

Mind

does
Witness
That-Which-Is

and
Imagine
What-Is-Not.

The
Realm
between
the
Two,

the
Surface...

There

the
Mind is caught.

Grasp
at
Water,

No water held.

Grasping Not,

Simply
Float.

Nothing

in which

Mind

can
Meld

but

Silence...

Eternal Note
.

28

Possibility

Some
States of affairs

could be
in
Time

as
they
are

**Not
Now,**

and

Some of those
Imagined

Pull

as
**Mind's One
Central Power**

.

Possibility

Remains

Unmeasured,

Shifting
Constantly

with
Ebbs and flows
of
Mind's Attention…

in
Patterns we call

Qi

.

29

In Voluntary

That much

of

the
World

we call
Our self...

that seems to

Follow Will,

the
Rest

we call
Other...

Divide and part and kill.

Yet...

The Student reminds us...

The boundary is arbitrary.

Having
Attended
the
Breath,

One Knows...

Divine

Now

Marry

.

Heart

Once believed

a
Simple pump
to keep
Blood flowing,

Now known
to
Be

So much more
Central to our Going.

Neurons... brain cells,

Therein do we find...

Electromagnetic fields

Toroidal in design.

Central
to the
Work,

its
Rhythms,

Guided
by
Breath...

Now fast,

Now slow,

Now rough,

Now smooth...

Attending Breath,

Heart follows.

The Student reminds us...

Groove

Groove

Groove

Entrainment

Two cycles
Similar enough

in their
Natural Groove,

Reducing beats
of
Texture rough,

Toward their Center move.

Universal Force
Pulls cycles
Close in Time.

Gravity
of
Temporal Space

Pulls rhythms toward their rhyme.

.
.
..
...
.....
....

Hearts entrain
to
Steady Breath

and

Hearts
to
One another.

Breath entrains
to
Attention,

Reflecting

Self in other

....
.....
...
..
.
.

Thus...

The Student remembers...

why
Virtue

is a
Must

for
One who seeks

to
Share

True Bread,

instead of
Molded crust.

Reflection

Imagine...

a
Long string
Tied firmly

to a
Wall,

Stretched taught

from
Your hand...

Sending a pulse along it...

watch the pulse

Reflect
at the
Boundary,

Traveling
back toward
its
Source,

Toward you...

Giving of itself

along
The Way.

Inspiring
All
that surrounds it
to
Dance.

What is a boundary

but where

Waves
Reflect
?

The Student remembers this image...

the
Sky

Seen

Looking down,

Sculpted by ripples

from a
Tossed pebble.

Where there is no pebble tossed,
No wind to blow...

What Ripple is It

that gives
Shape

to

Sky's
Reflecting
Glow
?

33

Boundary Conditions

A
Wave

Reflected

from a

Wall...

Surface...

Boundary...

Condition

that

the
Wave
be
Zero There

Boundary
Conditions

Form

the
Structures

amongst which

Move

the
Waves.

Reflections

amidst these

Structures...

Form
Patterns,

Echoes in caves.

34

Interference

Two
Pulses

Passing

each
Other

Do
Magic

as they
Meet
...

Combine

as
One

for a
Moment...

Both pointing up,

Form a greater,

Both down,

a
Greater
Too.

Opposing,

Lesser.

Equal and opposite,

Together
make
None
.

Interference Patterns

From

Two pebbles

Dropped

in the

Water

Emanate

Circular waves.

Waves

Crossing,

Interfere.

Adding,
Subtracting...

to and from
One another,

Forming

Some places greater,
Some places lesser...

Some places None,

New
Pattern

of the
Two as One,

from the
Couple
Born

...

Essence of Form.

Standing Waves

Wiggle

a
Cup
of
Water.

Waves

on the
Surface

Arise,

Reflecting

from the

Edges,

the
Boundary,

Criss-cross

Kaleidoscopically...

Interference symmetry.

The
Boundary conditions,

Shape
of the
Cup,

Determine

the
Lasting Forms
...

The Master asked...

When

is the

Middle

between

Now and then?

The Student answered...

Yes!

The Master said...

Where

is the

Middle

between

Here and there.

The Student responded...

Now

is the

Middle

between

Self and other

?

Modes

In

our
Cup

of

Water,

Symmetrical shapes

take
Form

at
Certain rates

of
Wiggle

.

Each

of
the

Possible Symmetries

Corresponds

to
a

Unique

Wiggling rate.

These Forms...

We call them each

a
Mode
.

Harmonics

A
Wave

on a
String

Fixed
at
Both ends

is

Zero

at

Certain

Points

.

.

The

Zero
Points

are

Bound to include

the
Ends

where

it

is

Fixed

. . . .
 . .
  .

How
Might

a
Symmetrical wave

on

a
String

Meet

these
Boundary conditions
?

The Student reminds us…

It is best

to

Discover

for our

Self

.

Sound

Pressure
Changes

in a
Gas

and

Tension
Shifts

in a
Body

Travel in waves...

much like
those that

We
Witness

on the
Surface of water
...

but...

with
One

Added dimension,

Radiating

in

All directions...

Layers of an onion.

As if...

Connected

by
Invisible springs,

the
Molecules

Bounce

Back and forth,

Pushing and pulling

on their

Neighbors

.

The
Sums

of

All

these
Rhythmic motions

Comprise

Wave
Forms...

of
Pressure...
Tension Variations.

These
Patterns

We call Sound.

Perceiving these... we hear.

Attending these... we Listen.

Hearing

Standing

in
the
Ocean,

the
Waves

Push and pull...

To and fro,
Back and forth

We

Go

.

We

Perceive

this
Slow vibration

throughout our

Body...

but

the
Waves

of
Pressure, tension,

that
We call Sound

are
Far too rapid
to
Feel

in
Such a way.

If
Too slow,

Sense
Nothing
at
All.

If
Fast enough,

Sense
a
Hum.

Now,

from
Silence

is
Born
Sound.

Perceiving
This,

We
Hear
.

Body Hearing

Slower hums

of

Sound,

We Hear

with
and
throughout

Our body,

where

Feeling and hearing

are

One

.

.
..
...
Sound felt

Illuminates
the
Shadows of Attention

in
Body space.

Wholeness

is

Restored

to
the

Illuminated pattern
.....
...
..
.

Regions
of
Body awareness,

Before divided,

Now

United as One
in the
Light of Attention,

Called forth

by

Sound felt,

where before

We

Felt

None

.

44

Ear Hearing

More

Subtle and rapid

Vibrations in air,

Perceived

with our
Sensitive ears...

Detailed geometries,

Proportions in Time

Comprise

the
Sound

that
We hear...

.
..
...

Patterns

Reflecting

from

All

that

Surrounds,

Continuous
Message

Encoded

as

Sound

...

..

.

Octave

As

We
Perceive
Sound

with
Body and ears,

a
Pattern emerges

within

the
Fluid framework

of
Feelings
Evoked

.

Imagine...

a

Simple wave
of
Pressure changes

Reaching us in air...

Pushing and pulling,

Rhythmic and steady,

Evoking
a
Certain feeling

far
Deeper
than
Words
.

Imagine...

another
wave

that
Pushes and pulls

at

Twice or half

the
Rate of the first...

somehow

Feels

the
Same

but also...

Different

.

The

Web of rates...

Twice or half
as
Rapid as the next...

Elemental structure
of
How
we
Feel

Sound,

We call this the Octave...

Fluid web
of
Sound perceived.

46

Tones & Notes

A
Simple steady pressure wave

Reaching us

just

Now...

perhaps

We Feel or hear

a
Hum...

with a
Certain flavor....

Not

to the
Tongue

.

Each

Frequency

of

Push and pull
on
Body and ears,

Its own special flavor

Identifies...

as do

Colors

to an

Eye

that

Sees

.

The

Feelings evoked

Identify

this
Frequency
or
That...

Faster or slower than another.

We call each flavor

a

Tone

and when

We give it a name,

We call that name

Note
.

Flavors of Tonal Spectrum

Imagine...

a

Tone...

It has

a

Certain flavor...

Indescribable in words.

.
..
...
.....
Another

Tone

of

Double or half
its
Frequency...

We call that...

One octave up
or
One down,

Respectively
....
.....
...
..
.

As

the

Second tone

Shares
some
Certain flavor
with the
First,

We call it

by the
Same name...

and

Distinguish the two
with a
Number...

like

$A_0 ...$ $A_1 ...$ $A_2 ...$ $A_3 ...$ A_∞

Between
Any two tones,

One
Double the other,

the
Octave Space

Rests pregnant
with
Tones

to

just

as
between
any

Here and there

are

Infinite possible points.

Infinite Tones

within

the

Octave

of
Flavors each unique

in
Relation
to
One
another
...

Comprise the tonal spectrum...

Colors or flavors

of

Sound
.

Divisions of Octave

The
Octave

from
One note
to a
Closest namesake,

Infinite
Spectrum
of
Tones,

we
divide
in
Patterns

so as to
Conceive its fluid slope

as
Simple quantized steps.

.
..
...
The

Continuous

Spectrum

Divided,

each
Piece

we
Give

a
Name

.

Just as

we
Divide

the
Continuous
Rainbow

into

a
Set

of
Discrete
Colors

and thus can

Say...

Blue,
Red,
or
Green,

.

we

likewise

Divide
the
Octave

into

a
Discrete set
of
Tones,

Each with a name;

the
Name

is

the
Note

.

49

Relativity of Frequency

.
.
..
...
.....
....
....

Frequencies

are

Relative,

Exist

Not

Alone

...
..
.

How many times

did

the
Wheel

Spin
Around

per

Cycle
of the
Clock?

How many cycles
Traversed

some
Mode of vibration

for each

Tik... Tok...

?

Assigning
Frequencies
to
Waves

is like

Assigning temperatures
to
One thing or another.

Hot or cold?

Relative to what?

Relative

to some state of the
Thermometer
we
choose...

and

Only relative.

Remember this.

Likewise

the
Frequency
of
Any cycle

is
Relative

to the

Tik-toks
Counted

by some
Clock.

What clock do you choose?

The
Chosen
Clock

Determines the frequency

as much as does

the
Wave
Itself

.

.
.
..
...
.....
Forgetting

this

Simple Truth...

Confusion

Arises.

Remembering...

Silence

Speaks

...

..

.

Intervals

That
Circle... Cycle

we call

the
Octave...

Flavor spectrum
of
Sound...

Feelings evoked

Traversing
its
Arc,

Somewhat repeat

as we go
Round

.

Dividing
the
Octave

into

a
Limited set

and

Labelling
each
Point

with

a
Name
we call
Note,

Compare
...

the
Space

between

any
Two
...

we call

an

Interval.

From
One
Note
to
Another,

How far do we jump?

How many steps

Round

the
Octave

?

.
..
...
Each

Interval,

each

Possible
Step,

These
are the
Real,

Not
Relative
...

Universal
...
..
.

.

As

Time and Space

Morph and melt

in
Relativity,

the
Intervals
yet
Remain.

Ratio...

Beginning
of
Heaven and Earth
.....
...
..
.

Whole Octave

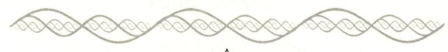

A
Step deeper...

Below

that
which can be
Named,
Identified,
or
Pointed out...

is

Ratio,
Eternal,

that
which
Evokes

those
Feelings arising
from
Sound

.

.
..
...
Even

the
Flavors,

Circular spectrum,

Spiraling
Inward and out...

that
we
call

the
Octave...

The Student reminds us...

those
Flavors

are each also
but
Relative,

having...

No

Substance

but

Relationship

to

One

another
...
..
.

No tone...
No note...

Exists
in
Isolation,

the
Whole

is

Composed
entirely of
Relationships...

Relationships
between
Relationships...

Wholeness
Beyond conception.

As
Lao Tzu reminds...

Darkness within *Darkness*...

Gateway
to all
Understanding

Chord & Scale Geometry

An
Interval,

a
Single jump,

from
One point
on the
Octave
to
another,

Defines
a
Side or segment

of

Geometries
within the
Octave,

those
Shapes

than can be

Inscribed
in the
Circle,

that
Set of points

where the

**Geometrical
Form**

Touches

the
Circle...

that...
we call

a

Scale
.

Rotate

that

Shape

within

the

Octave

and

the

Scale

is

Transposed...

Now
Touching
Different points.

.

Together

the
Sounds

Represented

by the

Points

of a

Geometry inscribed
within the
Octave circle

...

we call that set

a
Chord

...

a
Universal
Design

.

Harmony

.
...
.....
Nature
has
..
.
.
a
Way
...
..
.
.
Patterns
in
Form
.
we
Recognize

as
Beauty
.

Ever
Changing

to
Meet

the
Circumstance
That-Is,

It

cannot be

where
we
Point,

for

It

C   o   m es
and
go e   s

more
Quickly
than

any
Finger moves.

The

Living Beauty

of

Proportions

in every

Conceivable

Form...

That...

We

call

Harmony

·

Dancing

within
the

Octave...

ever
Responding

to
What
Now
Is,

the
Beauty

Takes
Shape

in

Ephemeral
Forms.

That
Dance
is
Life
Itself
.

Life

.
It
Is
Alive

.

What more can be said?

Perhaps...
a
Reminder

that

the
Boundary
between
Self and other

is

Arbitrary,
Relative,
Chosen

...

.

I
.
..
...
that

Circle

Dividing

All
That
Is

into

Self and other

....
....
...
..
.

The Student reminds us that...

Expanding

it
is
Endless.

Always

More lies beyond.

There
is

No
Path to Infinity

but

Dividing
by
Zero

•

One
Inconceivable
Step

and

All is One,
All is Alive.

Me?
You?
Who?

Stickiness

Will

Reflecting
upon
itself

becomes

Sticky
like
Glue,

Attaching

to

This, that,
or
Some other

Imagined
State
of
Affairs
.

A
Feedback
Loop

·

like
Mirrors
Reflecting
One
another.

Reflection
within
Reflection
within
Reflection
within
Reflection
within
Reflection
within
Reflection
within
Reflection

...
No
Apparent
Exit

·

Acknowledging this...

the
Student

Tries
Not to stick

and

Grows
ever more
Sticky
thereby.

That
Stickiness
is the
Trying
itself.

One choice remains...

Let go...

of

What

?

Health

Cooperating

in
Beautiful Harmony,

Webs
of
Dancing relationships,

Proportions
in
Every dimension…

Expressing

the
Song

we call

Life
…

Amidst

this
**Pervasive Dance
That**
is
All,

Will,

Turned
in on
Itself,

**Casts
Shadows**
of
Doubt and division,

Pathways...

where
Light of Attention

Appears
to
**Pass
Not**

.

Music

Draws
Together

in
Harmony

those
Patterned webs
of
Will.

Where
once seemed a
Shadow,

Exposed
as the
Light

is

that
Same Harmony

We call Life
.....
...
..
.
.

.
..
...
Health
...
..
.

.
..
...
.....
Expression
...
..
.
of
that
...
..
.
One

Dance

Eternal
...
..
.

Drone

Each
Place
we go,

we
only
Know

in
Relation
to
our
Home.

Once
Established,

a
Single Tone

forms the
Ground

on which
We Dance.

Every
Leap and twist

...

Transition

...

is
Known

only in
Relation

to

this
Ground.

That
Single Tone

on which
We Dance,

we call...

Drone

.

The Student remembered the Master...

     Seated
       so
     Still,

    Invisible
      to
     the
    Still Eye.

     for

     All
    that
     is
    Seen...

     is

    the
  Movement

   of the

    Eye
    that
    Sees

     .

Groove

.

The
Movements

of
the
Dance

Influence

O n e
another

as

Gravity

of

Form
through
Time
...
..
.

Steady
Rhythms
Repeating
Forms

in the
Dance of Life,

Draw

each
New movement

toward the

Forms...
Repeating
in
Time

as
Variations
and
Hints

of which

each
Movement

is a

Partial shadow cast.

This
Gravity

we call

Groove.

The Student remembered...

the
Dance

Tastes

Sweet

therein
.

Meditation

Attention and Will

Dance
as
Well.

Grooves
amidst
the
Dance of Form

offer
Invitation to Dance.

Invitation accepted,
Immersed
in the
Dance,
the
Dancer
is
Nowhere
to be
Found

.

The
Student
Forgot

the
Groove

that had
Caught

what once seemed
Will and Attention.

Though

the
Groove
Remains

...

Now is One

Here
to
Listen

?

60

Awakening

The Master asked...

Why is This so cryptic?

As
the
Student
Tried
to
Think
of an
Answer...

The Master interrupted...

That's why!

Treatment

Attention
on
the
Beauty,

the
Harmony

that is
Life
...

Expresses

in

Dance... Voice... Heart...
Breath... Thought... Feeling...

Radiating
Beautiful
Forms
...

Waves

in
every
Dimension

Invite All

to

the
Dance
that
is
Life.

Invitation
Accepted,

in
Song,
in
Dance,

the
Warmth of Welcome

we call

the
Energy of Life.

.
..
...

Invitation

both

Sent
and
Accepted...

this...

we call

Treatment

...

..

.

Language

Escaping
the
Grasps

of
every
Science...

Continue
so
It
shall...

nor
Expressed
in
Art
Alone

can
It
be
Captured
Whole
.

The
Strokes

of

Intuition's
Brush

are

too
Broad

for

It's
Fine detail.

The
Scans and divisions

of
Science

cannot
Express

how

it
Feels to Be

.

.
...
.....
....

neither

Art
nor
Science

Sufficient

to
Capture

this
Ephemeral Jewel,
....
....
....
.....
...
..
.
.

what
Language
might
we
Use
?

Indeed

we
have
the
Tool

...

Music
Itself

...

the
Language

that
Sings

of
That

...

Mother
of
both
Art and Science.

In Formation

Between

That
Which
Is

and

What
Might
Be,

a
Chasm

of

Changing Form,

we call
Information
.

Our
Story
...

we
Read

in

the
Movements

of

It's
Dance
.

```
          .
          .
         ..
         ...
        .....
       ........
      ............
    ......................
 ................................
```

The Student remembered That...

.

I

Am

the
Story

Reading

Itself

.

In Coding

Each
**Dancing
Form**

Sings
a
Song

as

Infinite

Modes
of
Vibration

Dancing

with

One
another
.

.
.....
That
Dance
of
Proportions

amidst

Infinite
Modes

Sings

to

All
That
Is

Telling
the
Life-story

of

the
One
who
Dances
....
.

The Student remembers That
....
....
....
....
.....
...
..
.
.
..
...
.....

Attention

is

that

Dance

...

..

.

Self

Visual Silence

.

Non-place

behind

your
Eyes,

Stillness

Beneath
every
Sense...

Pregnant
with
Possibility...

Fruit
of
Infinity

ever
Ripening...

Imagination

.

.

Beyond
Compare,

Silent,

Still,

Unknown
...

That

we
call
Self

.

The Student remembered...

The
Circle
of
No circumference

remains

Unfound

.

66

Is

Song

of

Itself

Singing

67
No Thing

is

Truth

Immersed

in

the
Song,

Dancing...

Imagination

Flowing
Freely

within the

Grooves

of

That
Which
Is,

.

The
Ruffled
Patterns

...

Beating
Waves

...

Born

of

the
Difference

between

Perception
and
Conception...

Growing
ever
Smoother,

Harmonize

.

Softly,

the
Ripples

Absorbing

One
another

Reveal
Stillness

...

Silent Center

in

the

Midst of Conditions

.

Honesty

The Student remembers...

Dancing
to
Silence
...

Singing to Stillness
...

and

calls

that

Honesty
.

70
Ethics

Attention

...

Dancing

to

the
Beautiful Song

...

Expresses

the
Harmony

That Is Life

in
Movements
of
Will

.

.
.
..
...
.....
....
....
Endearing

Each
to
All

...

this
Dance

we
call

Ethics

.

The Student remembers That...

the
Dance
Expresses
the
Song
as
the
Song
Expresses
the
Dance.

All
Movements
Radiating
their
Form,

Reflect and Return

One's
Story

as

One's
own
Reflection

.

Beauty All Around

is

the
Practice

is

Ethics

Community

.
..
...

Dancers

Dancing

within

Dances

of

Dancers

Dancing

...
..
.

The Student remembers That...

.

..

...

One

is

Born

of

Mother

.

..

.

Endeared

to
One
another

...

all
Dance...

Beautiful
Dance

.

Harmony

Expressing

Itself

...

..

.

..

...

.....

Beauty

Singing

that

Song

about

One Song Living

.

Waterfall Mountain

The Student remembered...

Waterfall

...

once
Frozen

...

Melted

.

Mountain

...

Eaten by Sky,

Simply passed away.

.

What
once
w a s

is

Now
Gone

into

Mists
of
Memory.

W h a t
s h a l l
be

Remains
Unknown

in

Shadows
that
None
See

.

.
..
...
......

Returning
to
that
Silent Center

...

..

.

Stillness

.

amidst

.

the
Dance

.

Mountain
Returns

.

Water
Flowing

.

Circle
Complete

....

.

Arriving

.

at
the
One
Center

...

Attention

both

Rests and Dances

Beautifully

.

???

Hand open Now,

Where has the fist gone?

That
Rate
between
Fast and slow...

What eyes see of themselves
with
No mirror...

The Student reminds us of...

the
Story
About
...

Completeness

The Student remembered...

.

Master

...

Saying Nothing

...

Left
Nothing
Out

.

Practice

The
Practice

is likened unto

Stacking sheets of paper.

So long does the Path appear,

Conceived as a series of steps.

.

So
Short

is
it
...

End
so
Near,

as

all
Steps

are

Known

to be

One

.

.
..
...
.....
....

Departing

...

Returning

...

with

every
Breath

...

Remember

...

the
Practice

is

Now

.

Student

After
many
Years

of

Devotion,
Study,
and
Practice,

The Student thought...

The Universe is All-That-Is...
and I... whatever I am...
am part of the Universe...
and I am experiencing
some part of the Universe.

Thus, I am
the
Universe
Experiencing Itself.

Yet
...

this
Thought

is

of
No
Avail

but

that

it
Leads
to
the
Practice
...

Returning to Returning
....
....
....
.....
...
..
.

77

Master

Perfection long forgotten,

the
Master

is

One

for
whom

All Is Now

the
Practice

.....

...

..

.

.

Cues & Keys

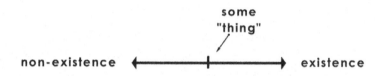

The 0ᵗʰ Dimension

The 1st Dimension is Born
X

The 2nd Dimension is Born
Y

The 3rd Dimension is Born
Z

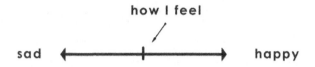

The Happy-Sad Dimension

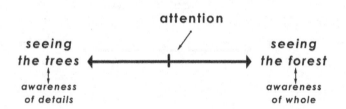

The Tree-Forest Dimension

Counting High-Fives at The Merry-Go-Round

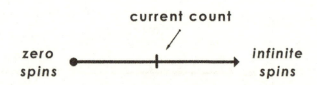

The Wheel-Spin Dimension

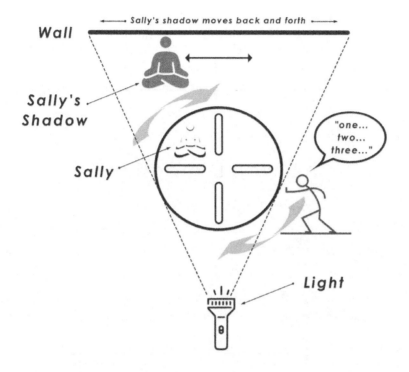

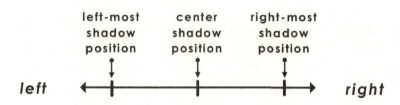

The Wall Dimension

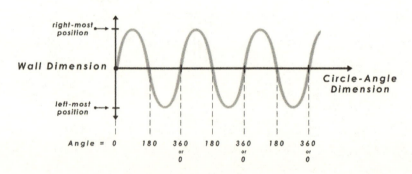

Shadow-Angle Game-Space

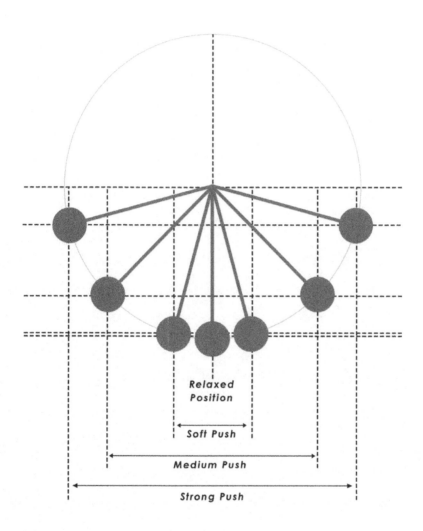

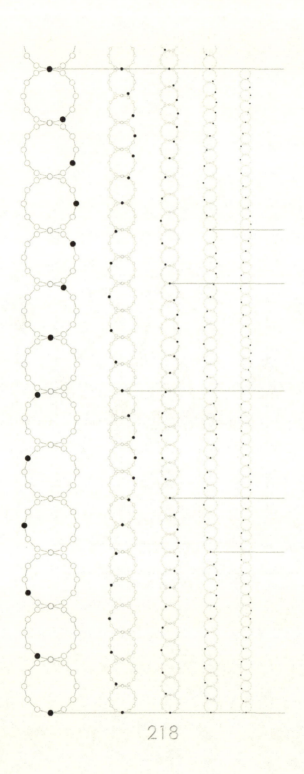

218

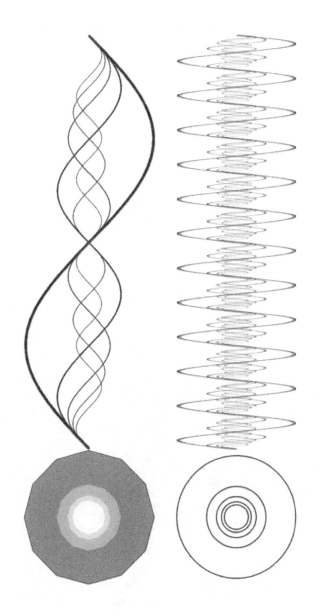

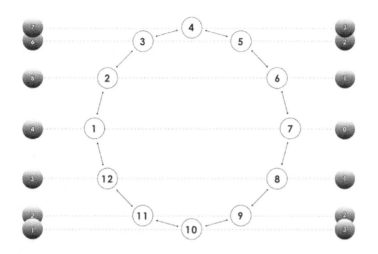
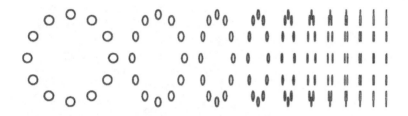
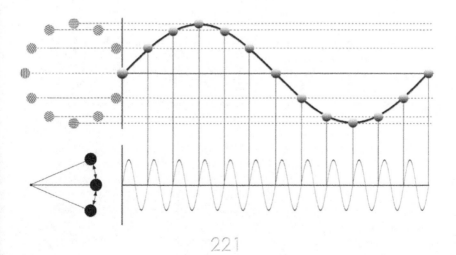

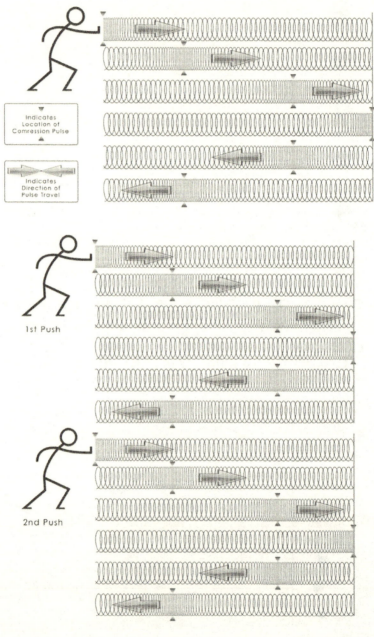

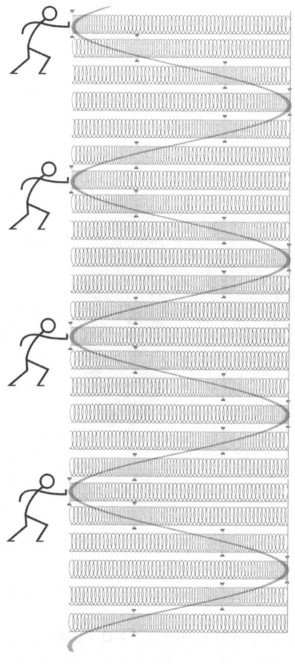

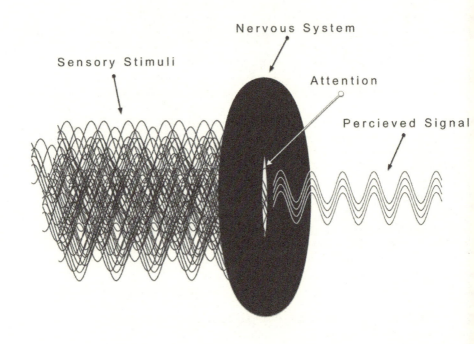

Attention as a Filter

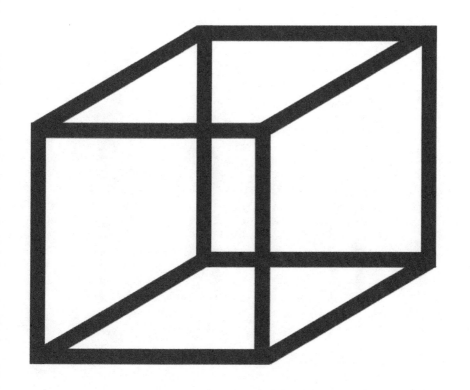

Choose Your Perspective

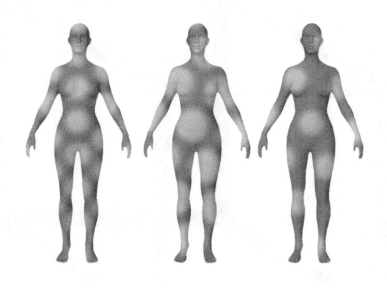

Isolated Regions of Attention
in
Body Space

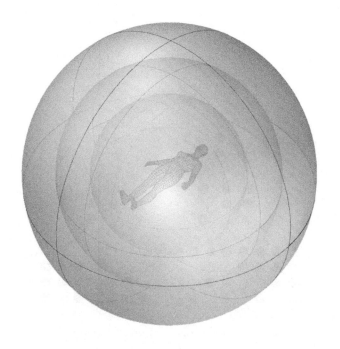

Attention Moves
through
Environmental Space

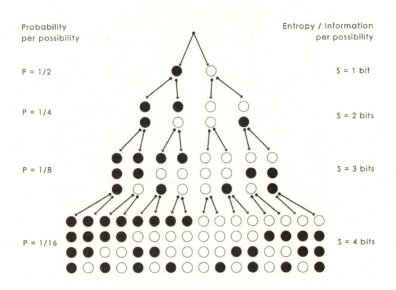

Shannon Information / Entropy
for simple coin toss

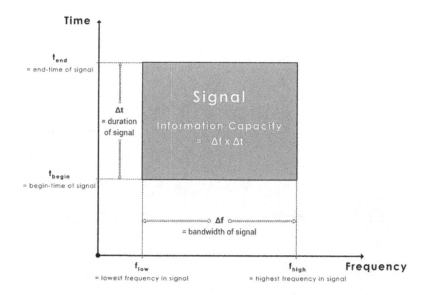

Gabor Information Capacity
of a
1-Dimensional Wave Signal

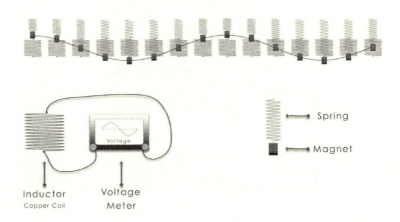

Producing an Oscillating Electrical Voltage
with
Magnet Hanging on a Spring
Passing through Copper Coil (Inductor)

Paper Diaphragm

Copper Coil
- Stiffly aatached to Diaphragm
- Connected to Varying Electrical Signal

Permanent Magnet

Varying Electrical Signal

Afterword

Having just completed the layout for the first edition, I thought it worthwhile to include something of a personal note to follow this dense and spacious text.

Particularly, I think it good to provide some glimpse into the reasoning behind this unusual format.

My perspective on Sound can be somewhat summarized as:

> *Before both Art and Science...*
>
> *Music is.*

This book is born from the above sentiment.

It is often wondered...

> *Why is the magic of Sound
> never fully captured in solely
> scientific or artistic grasps?*

I propose that this is for one simple reason...

> *Sound, or better yet Music...
> being Sound's Living Dance...
> is the Mother... the Root
> of both Art and Science.*

Neither Art nor Science can ever fully grasp Music.

Rather, it is in Music that we may fully grasp both Art and Science.

Music is fundamental... the essence of Nature... the essential foundation of all movement and form.

And it is for this very reason that Sound is Healing... for in the Dance of Sound that we call Music... therein do we find ourselves restored to Wholeness... the ground of Life.

This text is born from a continually deepening experience of the above... not as ideas, concepts, or beliefs... but as the Dance of my self that is the same Dance as that of All-That-Is.

That Dance

is

Music

.

Thus, this text is a poem... is Music.

Only in such a way might I perhaps trace a sufficient arc around the Silent Center so as to indicate Its location...

Everywhere and Nowhere.

May this book be a Gift to many for countless years to come.

with LOVE Truly,

- Thomas Orr Anderson
February 9, 2019
Sewanee, TN

About the Author

Books by author available on: *Amazon.com*

Explore his music at: *SiriusColors.com*

Learn more about his research, courses, workshops at: *PhiSonics.com*

Find his podcast on iTunes or SoundCloud:

   The Art and Science of Sound Healing

Join in the conversation on the Facebook group:

   The Art & Science of Sound Healing

To book the author for your event, email:

   Booking@ThomasOrrAnderson.com

The
Master
spoke...

When I hold up no fingers...

Clap.

The
Student
answered...

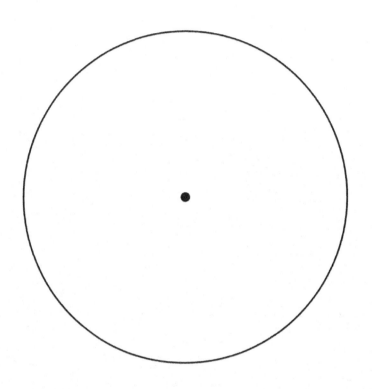

Master Handbook
of
Sound Healing

Made in United States
North Haven, CT
01 September 2023